Kumusta,
PHILIPPINES

by Corey Anderson

CHERRY LAKE PUBLISHING · ANN ARBOR, MICHIGAN

Published in the United States of America by Cherry Lake Publishing
Ann Arbor, Michigan
www.cherrylakepublishing.com

Reading Adviser: Marla Conn MS, Ed., Literacy specialist, Read-Ability, Inc.

Book Design: Book Buddy Media

Photo Credits: ©iStockphoto/Getty Images, cover (top); ©EyeEm/Getty Images, cover (bottom); ©EyeEm/Getty Images, 1; ©Stockbyte/Getty Images, 3; ©John Seaton Callahan/Getty Images, 4; ©pop_jop/Getty Images, 6; ©Nikada/Getty Images, 7; ©John Seaton Callahan/Getty Images, 8; ©EyeEm/Getty Images, 9; ©Yla Corotan/Wikimedia, 10; ©EyeEm/Getty Images, 11; ©kormandallas/Pixabay, 12; ©ICHAUVEL/Getty Images, 13; ©EyeEm/Getty Images, 14; ©iStockphoto/Getty Images, 16; ©Karl Tapales/Getty Images, 17; ©Chris Dela Cruz/Getty Images, 18 (top); ©bgblue/Getty Images, 18 (bottom); ©National Museum of the U.S. Navy/Wikimedia, 19; ©EyeEm/Getty Images, 20; ©saiko3p/Shutterstock, 21; ©Josep Gutierrez/Getty Images, 22; ©Gilbert Rondilla Photography/Getty Images, 23; ©Jekaterina Nikitina/Getty Images, 24; ©icewater photography/Getty Images, 25; ©Gilbert Rondilla Photography/Getty Images, 26; ©Prawny/Pixabay, 27; ©Robertus Pudyanto/Getty Images, 28; ©jhorrocks/Getty Images, 29; ©How Foo Yeen/Getty Images, 30; ©Mariano Sayno / husayno.com/Getty Images, 31; ©iStockphoto/Getty Images, 32; ©iStockphoto/Getty Images, 33; ©maryaddison80/Pixabay, 35; ©aldarinho/Shutterstock, 36; © h3k27/Getty Images, 37; ©EyeEm/Getty Images, 38; ©iStockphoto/Getty Images, 39; © Sergio Amiti/Getty Images, 40; ©iStockphoto/Getty Images, 41; ©iStockphoto/Getty Images, 42; ©kawalingpinoy/Wikimedia, 43; ©Hendrasu/Shutterstock, 44; ©Sergio Amiti/Getty Images, 45

Copyright ©2020 by Cherry Lake Publishing
All rights reserved. No part of this book may be reproduced or utilized in any form
or by any means without written permission from the publisher.

Library of Congress Cataloging-in-Publication Data has been filed and is available at catalog.loc.gov

Cherry Lake Publishing would like to acknowledge the work of The Partnership for 21st Century Learning.
Please visit www.p21.org for more information.

Printed in the United States of America

TABLE OF CONTENTS

CHAPTER 1

WELCOME TO THE PHILIPPINES!

Palawan Island is the fifth-largest island in the Philippines. It has white sandy beaches and stunning mountainsides.

Imagine a country where an incredible variety of exotic plants, colorful birds, and beautiful beaches are found not far from busy cities where millions of people live. A place where warm and often rainy weather means you'll sometimes need an umbrella, but rarely a winter coat. That's the Philippines! Located in Southeast Asia, the Philippines is an **archipelago**, which means it is made up of many individual islands. In fact, the Philippines is made up of more than 7,000 islands, big and small! Although many of the islands are uninhabited, which means humans do not live on them, there are countless interesting towns, cities, coastlines, and forests to explore in this fascinating country.

ACTIVITY

Although there are more than 7,000 islands that make up the Philippines, most maps show a lot fewer. Trace the islands you see here. Label Manila. Use an atlas or find a map online that will help you label the three main groups of islands: Luzon, the Visayas, and Mindanao. Label Mount Mayon and Mount Pinatubo too. These are two famous volcanoes.

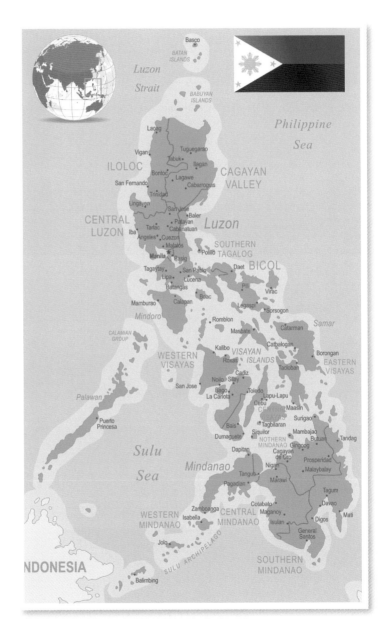

Manila is the largest city in the Philippines and its capital city. It is located on the island of Luzon, which is the Philippines' biggest island by size and population. Millions of people live in Manila, packed into a bustling **metropolis** known for its contrasts. Fancy hotels and malls are found next to hectic street-food markets and stately old Spanish colonial buildings. With a wide variety of restaurants, shopping, and things to do in the city's entertainment zones, Manila offers tourists a dazzling array of things to explore and see.

The city of Manila's Chinatown is the world's oldest, built in the 1500s. It is where many Filipino people go to buy Chinese goods and eat Chinese food.

Since it is entirely made up of islands, the Philippines has one of the longest coastlines of any country in the world. Miles of white, pristine beaches and dazzling light blue and green ocean water make the Philippines a popular place for people who like to dip their toes in the sand or spot marine life. The country is also very mountainous. The tallest peak is Mount Apo, which is 9,692 feet (2,954 meters) high.

The Philippines and the Ring of Fire

The Philippines is part of the Ring of Fire, which is a horseshoe-shaped line of volcanoes and sites of earthquakes around the edge of the Pacific Ocean. Earthquakes hit the Philippines fairly frequently, with the largest being the Moro Gulf earthquake of 1976, which hit a magnitude of 7.9 out of 10. In December of 2018, a 7.1 earthquake hit the Davao region of the Philippines.

Street markets and sidewalk shopping booths in the Philippines offer everything from clothes to discounted jewelry to food.

Although many of the country's islands are **undeveloped**, millions of people live very close to one another in the Philippines' most crowded cities, including Manila. On average, Manila has 36,000 people per square mile, making it one of the most crowded cities on Earth. In the city's slums, there are more than there are 200,000 people per square mile, packed into shacks and other poor housing conditions. People in slums often deal with problems like crime and unclean living conditions.

More than 100 million people live in the Philippines, even though it's actually a very small country. If you put all the islands together, it would be about the size of Arizona!

The Philippines is considered tropical, which means it is very hot and humid all year. March through June is the hottest and driest time of year. The typhoon season in the Philippines is June through December. A typhoon is an extremely heavy rainstorm that can cause landslides and other problems for residents.

Inside the Walls of Intramuros

There's a walled city in the center of Manila called Intramuros. Intramuros means "inside the walls." Built in the 1500s to protect the city from invaders, it also originally housed the Spanish government officials who ruled over the city. Although it was almost completely destroyed by the end of World War II (1939–1945), many of the buildings have since been rebuilt, and its ancient walls still stand today.

Compared to the size of their bodies, tarsiers have the largest eyes of any mammal.

From peaceful whale sharks and bright purple crabs, to tiny primates with giant eyes known as tarsiers, many unusual animals can be found in the seas and land of the Philippines. The Philippines is a country known for its biodiversity, which means a wide variety of animals call its islands their home. Unfortunately, many animals in the Philippines are now **endangered**, including the Philippine eagle, Visayan warty pig, and the Philippine tarsier.

Five of the seven different species of sea turtles live in the Philippines.

New Discoveries

Over a 15-year study in the 2000s, scientists discovered 28 new mammal species on the island of Luzon in the Philippines. These mammals are all endemic to the country, which means they are not found anywhere else in the world. The animals that were discovered all can be classified as types of rodents called cloud rats and earthworm mice.

CHAPTER 2

BUSINESS AND GOVERNMENT IN THE PHILIPPINES

For the majority of the country's history, most people in the Philippines earned a living by farming or fishing. The islands' rich, volcanic soil has always been excellent for growing crops. Foods like corn, coconut, sugarcane, bananas, and pineapples have been grown by farmers across the country for many years.

The Banaue rice terraces were created more than 2,000 years ago. They are still used to grow rice today.

Crops as diverse as peanuts, cassava, rubber, and cotton are also grown in the Philippines.

The Philippines' agricultural products come from four categories: farming, fisheries, livestock, and forestry. Many people in the country still live in **rural** areas, and about 26 percent of the country's workers have jobs supporting agriculture. Nearly 50 percent of the land of the Philippines is used for agriculture!

The Philippines has other industries outside of agriculture. People who work in factories produce machinery, computers, boats, and vehicles. Those items either remain in the country for citizens to purchase and use or they are **exported**. To export a good or product means to ship it to another country for purchase by others around the world.

TOP EXPORTS FROM THE PHILIPPINES

Electrical machinery and equipment: **$28.4 billion**

Machinery, including computers: **$9.4 billion**

Optical, technical, and medical apparatus: **$2.6 billion**

Copper: **$2.1 billion**

Ships and boats: **$1.7 billion**

Animal and vegetable fats, oils, and waxes: **$1.6 billion**

Wood: **$1.4 billion**

Gems and precious metals: **$1.4 billion**

Fruits and nuts: **$1.2 billion**

Vehicles: **$1.2 billion**

| 0 | 10% | 20% | 30% | 40% | 50% |

Imports and exports out of the Philippines often pass through the busy Port of Manila shipping container terminals.

The Philippines **imports** products from all over the world, which means goods are brought into the country from elsewhere. Around 80 percent of the items that are imported into the Philippines come from other countries in Asia. Machinery, fuels, vehicles, and natural resources like iron and steel are the top things imported into the country.

ACTIVITY

A pie chart is one way to compare data. In the Philippines, about 56 percent of workers provide services. About 26 percent have jobs related to agriculture. Approximately 18 percent have jobs related to industry. And about 6 percent have other types of jobs. Using this labor force information, create a pie chart. Ask an adult for help if you need it.

Shoemaking in the Philippines

The Philippines' City of Marikina was once one of the leading centers for shoemaking in Southeast Asia. In the early 2000s, it began to decline when cheaper shoes started being imported from China. But in recent years, thanks to social-media advertising and online sales, Marikina's shoe sales have increased. As of 2017, sales had risen 85% since 2010.

The Marcos Hall of Justice is a courthouse located in Laoag City, in the northern part of the Philippines.

The Spanish-American War

Parts of the Spanish-American War were fought in the Philippines. After the United States won the war, the United States decided to give Spanish-ruled Cuba its independence, but kept control of the Philippines, which helped establish the United States as a world power.

The government in the Philippines is a republic. People in the Philippines elect a president. Unlike the 4-year term of the U.S. president, the Filipino president serves for 6 years.

On May 1, 1898, the United States fought Spain in the Battle of Manila Bay. This led to the fall of the Philippines, and ultimately, the United States winning the war.

The explorer Ferdinand Magellan arrived in the Philippines in the 1500s. Soon after, the country became a Spanish colony. The Spanish ruled the country for hundreds of years. After the Spanish-American War in 1898, the United States took over control of the Philippines, but the country started governing itself in the mid-1930s.

On New Year's Eve in Manila, beautiful fireworks displays are set off all over the city.

The Philippines gained full independence in 1946, when it became the Republic of the Philippines. In 1965, Ferdinand Marcos was elected president and soon declared a dictatorship. Marcos was forced out of office in 1986, and **democracy** took over again.

President Maria Corazon

After the dictatorship of Ferdinand Marcos fell in 1986, Maria Corazon Aquino became president of the Philippines. She became the first female president of the country and brought democracy back to the nation.

Today, the power of the Filipino government is equally divided between the executive, legislative, and judicial branches. The executive branch is where the president sits, the legislative branch makes the country's laws, and the judicial branch helps to enforce its laws.

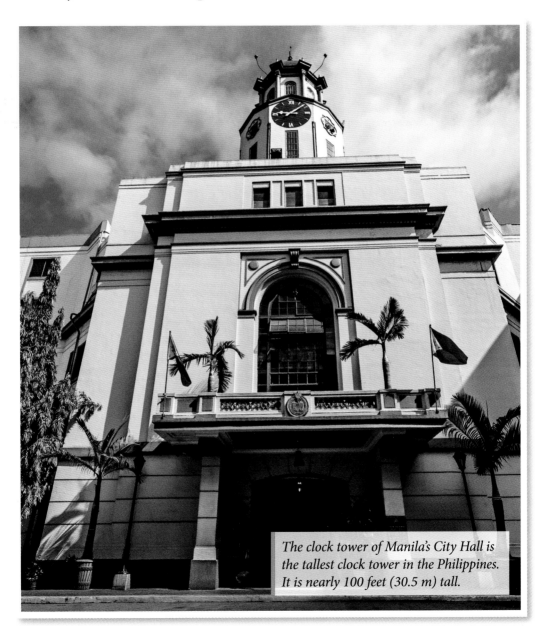

The clock tower of Manila's City Hall is the tallest clock tower in the Philippines. It is nearly 100 feet (30.5 m) tall.

CHAPTER 3

MEET THE PEOPLE

People have lived on the land that eventually became the Philippines for thousands of years. Scientists think that a bridge of land may have once connected the Philippines to Asia. That means people would have been able to migrate from mainland Asia to the Philippines by walking! Groups started arriving in the Philippines more than 30,000 years ago.

Many Filipinos today are part Malay, as their ancestors traveled to the Philippines originally by boat from Malay and Indonesian islands.

The people of the Philippines as a whole are called Filipinos. But when talking about women specifically, they are called Filipinas.

The Philippines is often considered to be one of the friendliest countries in the world.

There are more than 180 languages spoken in the Philippines. Of these, 175 languages come from the native populations of the country. Most people in the country speak English or Tagalog. Tagalog is thought of as the basis of the country's national language, which is taught as "Filipino" in schools today.

Today, the Philippines is a melting pot of people from around the world. For hundreds of years, people from other countries have come to live in the Philippines. Settlers from Europe, India, and China often married people from the Philippines, creating people of blended ethnicities, called mestizos.

The beautiful crescent-shaped Dahican Beach is very popular with surfers and families.

Spanish was introduced to people in the Philippines in the 1500s. And even though Spain controlled the Philippines for hundreds of years, the people never fully adopted Spanish as their primary language. People ultimately chose Tagalog and English. There is a push now for people to learn Spanish because much of the country's historical documents are written in the language.

ENGLISH	TAGALOG
Hello or How are you?	Musta (informal)
Long time no see!	Tagal na ah!
What's your name?	Anong pangalan mo?
My name is . . .	Ang pangalan ko ay . . .
Thank you	Salamat

In the Philippines, a palengke *is the term for a public market with several stalls where locals sell goods and foods like fresh vegetables.*

In the Philippines, the school year typically begins in June and ends in March.

Children in the Philippines used to only have to go to school for 10 years. New laws in the early 2000s made it mandatory for kids to go to school for 13 years, similar to the kindergarten through 12th grade system used in the United States. Kids across the country are typically taught in both Tagalog and English, learning both of the country's official languages throughout their studies. In their first years of schooling, students learn about *makabayan*, which focuses on developing a healthy personal and national identity.

ACTIVITY

In the Philippines, the Sarimanok is a legendary bird. It is often shown with wings and a feathered tail, holding a fish. The Sarimanok is also shown with leaves and scrolls on its head.

TO MAKE YOUR OWN SARIMANOK:

1. Draw a pattern of the bird's body on a piece of cardboard.
2. Cut out the outline.
3. Cut out strips of tissue paper in yellow, purple, and green.
4. Glue the strips onto the bird's body, starting from the tail. These are the bird's feathers.
5. Continue to add colorful strips until the bird's whole body is covered in feathers.

In the Philippines, the Sarimanok bird is considered to be a symbol of good fortune.

In 1975, the Philippine Basketball Association was created. It was the first professional basketball league established outside of the United States.

Many sports are popular in the Philippines, but the sport loved most across the country is basketball. The national team is called Gilas Pilipinas, and the team competes against other countries in international competitions. Boxing is also beloved in the Philippines. A Filipino named Manny Pacquiao is one of the best boxers in the world. *Dumog* and *sikaran* are traditional sports played in the country. They are forms of wrestling and kickboxing.

In the Philippines, a style of kickboxing called Yaw-Yan *is popular.* Yaw-Yan *means "Dance of Death."*

Manny Pacquiao, Sports Legend

Boxing is beloved across the Philippines, and Manny Pacquiao is a national legend in the country. He is considered one of the best athletes to come from the Philippines. Between 1998 and 2010, he won boxing titles in eight different weight classes, from flyweight at 112 pounds (50.8 kilograms) to junior middleweight at 144 pounds (65.3 kg). Pacquiao's nickname is "Pac-Man." He eventually starred in movies and TV shows in the Philippines, and even served in politics.

CELEBRATIONS

Filipinos celebrate many different holidays, with fiestas being held across the country throughout the year. Every town or village hosts a fiesta to celebrate patron saints and to honor the changing of the seasons. People believe their patron saint protects their town. The fiestas usually are filled with delicious food, music, and parades. Filipinos also love Christmastime. The Christian holiday is widely celebrated throughout the country.

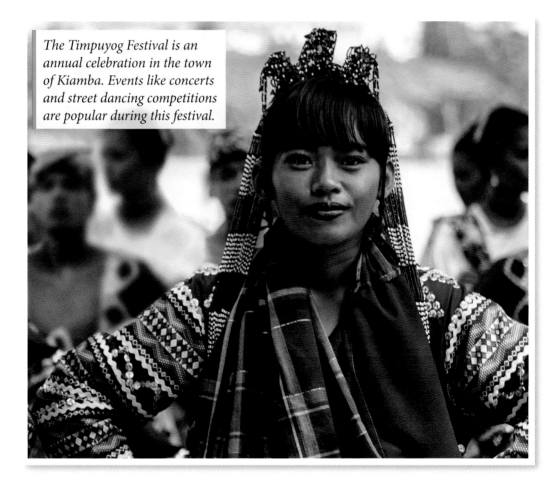

The Timpuyog Festival is an annual celebration in the town of Kiamba. Events like concerts and street dancing competitions are popular during this festival.

Christianity and Islam are the two main religions observed in the Philippines. Islamic traders from the Middle East and India helped to spread the religion across the Philippines. Today, around 5 percent of Filipinos practice Islam. The majority of Filipinos are Christian and practice Catholicism specifically. Spanish **missionaries** introduced Christianity to the Philippines in the 1500s, and over time, many Filipinos converted to the religion.

During Holy Thursday and Good Friday, many Filipinos practice Visita Iglesia, *in which they visit at least seven different Catholic churches on Holy Thursday and Good Friday.*

CELEBRATIONS AND HOLIDAYS

These are some holidays that are celebrated in the Philippines:

New Year's Day - January 1

Holy Thursday - March or April

Good Friday - March or April

Easter Sunday - March or April

Labor Day - May 1

Independence Day - June 12

Filipino-American Friendship Day - July 4

Hari-Raya Poasa - end of Ramadan

Bonifacio Day - November 30

Christmas - December 25

Rizal Day - Monday nearest December 30

In addition to their own unique traditions around the holiday, Filipinos also put up Christmas trees, sing Christmas carols, and get visits from Santa Claus.

ACTIVITY

Try making your own *boka-boka* kite.

MATERIALS

- 1 sheet of paper, 8.5 inches by 11 inches (22 centimeters by 28 cm)
- crayons or markers
- thread
- string
- tape
- a pencil
- a ruler
- scissors

INSTRUCTIONS

1. Lay the piece of paper on a flat work surface, with one of the shorter sides closest to you. Using a pencil, label the shorter side farthest from you "A." Label the shorter side closest to you "B." Label the long side to the left "C" and the long side to the right "D."

2. Decorate the paper however you like using crayons or markers.

3. Place your paper in front of you, with the decorated side facing up and side B closest to you.

4. Take a ruler and measure 2.5 inches (6.4 cm) from the edge of side B. Draw a line parallel to side B across your paper at that point. Draw another parallel line 2.5 inches (6.4 cm) from side A.

5. Fold your paper along each of these lines, so that the A and B labels are folded under and facing the tabletop.

6. Turn your paper over so that the decorated side is facedown. Side C should be closest to you.

7. Start with the left-hand flap. Measure 2.5 inches (6.4 cm) up from the edge of side C. Mark this spot with a pencil. Repeat this step with the right-hand flap.

8. Using scissors, cut a piece of thread that is 44 inches (112 cm) long.

9. Tape one end of the thread to the left-hand pencil mark. Tape the other end to the right-hand pencil mark. You should now have a loop of string attached to the kite.

10. Turn your kite over.

11. Cut a piece of string that is 5 feet (1.5 m) long.

12. Thread this piece of string through the loop that's attached to the kite. This will be what you hold onto as you fly the kite. Tie the ends of the string into a knot.

13. You are now ready to fly your kite!

Kite-flying in the Philippines is a popular activity for families to do together.

Mosques in the Philippines are often beautiful, brightly colored structures with elaborate designs.

Muslims also have important religious holidays. After the holy time of Ramadan, Filipino Muslims celebrate Hari-Raya Poasa. They pray and enjoy time with family.

During festivals, Filipinos often wear bright, beautiful traditional clothing. Men wear a special **embroidered** shirt called a *barong tagalog*. Women might wear a dress called a *terno* or a long skirt known as a *saya*.

For fun, kids in the Philippines play games, or they might go out and fly a boka-boka, which is a small kite.

In the Philippines, folk dances in traditional clothing are popular celebrations of Filipino culture. The dances are often passed down from generation to generation.

CHAPTER 5

WHAT'S FOR DINNER?

The food of the Philippines is often a reflection of the diversity of its people. Filipino **cuisine** gets its flavors and cooking styles from all over the world. Influences of Spain, China, Southeast Asia, and the United States are found in street food and in the dishes served around the family dinner table.

Popular flavors and spices in the Philippines include coconut, garlic patis *(a salty fish sauce), vinegar, and* bagoong *(a flavorful shrimp or rfish paste).*

No matter what you're eating, you're likely to find rice on your plate. Instead of side dishes like corn or potatoes, nearly all foods in the Philippines are served with rice. And if there's leftover rice after a meal, it's often combined with spices and other ingredients to make a new dish.

Desserts in the Philippines

Filipinos often end their meals with a sweet treat. A popular Filipino dessert is *halo-halo*, which means "mix mix." It is a mix of sweet ingredients like fruit, coconut, or Jell-O on top of a starchy base like beans. Ice creams in the Philippines come in many unusual flavors as well, and they are often very colorful. Mango, jackfruit, avocado, and *ube*, a purple yam, are common ice cream flavors to enjoy in the Philippines.

For people who enjoy Asian flavors but don't like spicy foods, Filipino cuisine is often a great find. Unlike other Asian cuisines, Filipinos don't add hot peppers to as many dishes. Besides the staple of rice, other common ingredients in Filipino foods include corn, bread, and noodles. Those types of ingredients can be used across many different types of cooking styles.

Lunch in the Philippines is often a simple noodle dish, served with seafood or meat.

Grilling seafood like fish, shrimp, and lobster is a popular cooking method in the Philippines.

Given that it's an island nation, it's also no surprise that Filipino dishes feature the seafood of the area, with tilapia, bass, clams, and shrimp appearing as protein in dishes. Pork and chicken are also commonly used, while beef is used less frequently.

Chicken *adobo* might be the best-known Filipino dish. *Adobo* is the Spanish word for marinade, so the dish features chicken marinated in a mixture of soy sauce and vinegar. Other hearty dishes include *kare-kare*, a stew made with peanut sauce, which is often served up with fermented seafood paste on the side. *Lechon*, or a fully roasted pig, is a delicacy enjoyed at fiestas and other special occasions.

Street Treats

Street food is a big part of the culture in the Philippines. Popular street foods in the country include *kwek-kwek*, which are deep fried quail eggs, or *taho*, a fresh bean curd that is sweetened by caramelized brown sugar. *Buko* juice, or the water from a freshly cut coconut, is a refreshing accompaniment to any savory street treat.

RECIPE

Maja blanca is a sweet coconut pudding that is a popular dessert in the Philippines. Often, it will have small pieces of corn inside or will be topped with flakes of coconut.

INGREDIENTS

- 1/2 cup (125 milliliters) water
- 1/2 cup (64 grams) cornstarch
- 1 cup (250 ml) coconut milk
- 3/4 cup (180 ml) water
- 1/2 cup (100 g) white sugar
- 1/4 cup (59 ml) fresh sweet corn kernels
- 1/4 cup (21 g) sweetened flaked coconut

INSTRUCTIONS

1. Grease an 8-inch (20-cm) baking dish or pie pan. Set aside.
2. Mix 1/2 cup (125 ml) of water with the cornstarch in a bowl. Stir until smooth.
3. Combine the coconut milk, 3/4 cup (180 ml) of water, and sugar in a saucepan over low heat, and stir until the sugar is dissolved.
4. Bring the mixture to a boil.
5. Add the corn kernels, and then stir in the cornstarch mixture, stirring quickly to avoid lumps as it becomes thick.
6. Bring the mixture back to a boil and simmer until fully thickened and smooth. Make sure to stir constantly.
7. Pour the mixture into the prepared dish. Set aside to cool until firm, about 2 hours.
8. Place the coconut flakes in a dry skillet over medium heat and stir to toast. Watch them carefully so they don't burn.
9. Remove the toasted coconut flakes to a bowl and let cool.
10. Sprinkle over the pudding before serving.

On a typical day, it's common for Filipinos to eat five small meals. They start with an early breakfast, which is followed up by a mid-morning snack, which is called *merienda*. After lunch, Filipinos enjoy a late afternoon snack before dinner. Sometimes, appetizers are even served before dinner. People will finish the day with sweets or fruit, with coconut and caramel being common ingredients in desserts.

Sweetened bananas, called Minatamis na Saging, *are a common dessert in the Philippines.*

Beaches are a common destination for Filipino families to spend an outing together.

The Philippines is a lush, beautiful place that island lovers and city dwellers alike will love. For a rich culture filled with vibrant celebrations, delicious foods, and warm people, the Philippines is an amazing place to visit.

GLOSSARY

archipelago *(ar-kuh-PEL-uh-goh)* a large group or chain of islands

cuisine *(kwi-ZEEN)* a style or way of cooking or presenting food

democracy *(dem-AHK-ruh-see)* a political system in which the people elect leaders to represent them in government

embroidered *(em-BROI-dur-ee)* cloth which has designs stitched into it

endangered *(en-DAYN-jurd)* at risk of dying out completely

exported *(EK-spor-ted)* sold and shipped to another country

imports *(IM-port)* brings in from another country

metropolis *(meh-TRAH-puh-liss)* a large, important, densely populated city

missionaries *(MISH-uh-ner-eez)* people sent by a religious group to teach their faith in a foreign country

rural *(RUR-uhl)* having to do with the country or farming

undeveloped *(un-duh-VEHL-upd)* land not used for living, farming, or any other industry

FOR MORE INFORMATION

BOOKS

Bankston, John. *We Visit the Philippines.* Your Land and My Land: Asia. Hockessin, DE: Mitchell Lane Publishers, 2014.

Burgan, Michael. *Philippines.* Countries Around the World. Chicago, IL: Heinemann Library, 2014.

WEB SITES

Britannica—The Philippines
https://www.britannica.com/place/Philippines
Learn more about the Philippines and its people, economy, government, and more in this informative article by Britannica.

Digital Dialects—Filipino Language Games
http://www.digitaldialects.com/Filipino.htm
Learn and practice Filipino words and phrases with these interactive games.

National Geographic Kids—Philippines
https://kids.nationalgeographic.com/explore/countries/philippines/
Read more about the history, government, and culture of the Philippines.

INDEX

ABOUT THE AUTHOR

Corey Anderson is a writer and editor based in the Los Angeles area. When not typing away at a computer, Corey enjoys exploring Southern California with her two sons and husband, and participating in running races and other athletic pursuits.